Ready for School

Katie Peters

GRL Consultant Diane Craig,
Certified Literacy Specialist

Lerner Publications ◆ Minneapolis

Note from a GRL Consultant
This Pull Ahead leveled book has been carefully designed for beginning readers.
A team of guided reading literacy experts has reviewed and leveled the book to
ensure readers pull ahead and experience success.

Lerner Publications
An imprint of Lerner Publishing Group, Inc.
241 First Avenue North
Minneapolis, MN 55401 USA

For reading levels and more information, look up this title at www.lernerbooks.com.

Main body text set in Memphis Pro 24/39
Typeface provided by Linotype.

Photo Acknowledgments
The images in this book are used with the permission of: © artisteer/iStockphoto, p. 3;
© kali9/iStockphoto, pp. 4–5; © monkeybusinessimages/iStockphoto, pp. 6–7, 10–11,
14–15, 16 (book, bus); © FatCamera/iStockphoto, pp. 8–9; © SDI Productions/iStockphoto,
pp. 12–13, 16 (pencil).

Front Cover: © shaunl/iStockphoto

Library of Congress Cataloging-in-Publication Data

Names: Peters, Katie, author.
Title: Ready for school / by Katie Peters.
Description: Minneapolis : Lerner Publications, 2024. | Series: Let's look at fall. Pull ahead
    readers—nonfiction | Includes index. | Audience: Ages 4–7 | Audience: Grades K–1 |
    Summary: "The first day of school is very exciting with so many new things to do. Engage
    emergent readers with full-color photographs and easy-to-read text. Pairs with the
    fiction title Let's Go to School"— Provided by publisher.
Identifiers: LCCN 2022033547 (print) | LCCN 2022033548 (ebook) | ISBN 9781728491295
    (library binding) | ISBN 9798765603161 (paperback) | ISBN 9781728498065 (ebook)
Subjects: LCSH: First day of school—Juvenile literature.
Classification: LCC LB1556 .P47 2024 (print) | LCC LB1556 (ebook) | DDC 372.21—dc23/
    eng/20220818

LC record available at https://lccn.loc.gov/2022033547
LC ebook record available at https://lccn.loc.gov/2022033548

Manufactured in the United States of America
1 – CG – 7/15/23

Table of Contents

Ready for School

We start school in the fall.

Many things are new.

We get on the bus.

We meet our new driver.

We go to the classroom.
We meet our new teacher.

We read new books.

We write with new pencils.

We go to recess.

We make new friends!

How do you get ready for school?

Did You See It?

book

bus

pencil

Index